I0419667

Wicca:
The Ultimate Beginners Guide For Witches and Warlocks

Learn Wicca Magic Spells, Traditions and Rituals

By

Michele Gilbert

Visit My Amazon Author Page

Dedicated to those who choose to stretch beyond their own limits and to seek a more abundant and fulfilling life.

Your thoughts are creative.

Michele Gilbert

My Free Gift To You!

As a way of saying thank you for downloading my book, I am willing to give you access to a selected group of readers who (every week or so) receive inspiring, life-changing kindle books at deep discounts, and sometimes even absolutely free.

Wouldn't it be great to get amazing Kindle offers delivered directly to your inbox?

Wouldn't it be great to be the first to know when I'm releasing new fresh and above all sharply discounted content?

But why would I so something like this?

Why would I offer my books at such a low price and even give them away for free when they took me countless hours to produce?

Simple…. Because I Want To Spread The Word!

For a few short days Amazon allows Kindle authors to promote their newly released books by offering them deeply discounted (up to 70% price discounts and even for free. This allows us to spread the word extremely quickly allowing users to download thousands and thousands of copies in a very short period of time.

Once the timeframe has passed, these books will revert back to their normal selling price. That's why you will benefit from being the first to know when they can be downloaded for free!

So are you ready to claim your weekly Kindle books?

You are just one click away! Follow the link below and sign up to start receiving awesome content

Thank you and Enjoy!

Table of contents

Introduction

I want to thank you and congratulate you for downloading the book, *Wicca: The Ultimate Guide For Witches and Warlocks*.

This book contains proven steps and strategies on how to get the truth on what Wicca is all about and a peek inside the Craft.

Sure, there are a lot of TV shows out there and movies that have to do with Wicca or have Wiccans in them, but is it all true? What does it really mean to actually cast spells? I mean, science is a thing and it says that it's not possible, right? Right?!

Well, the truth is, we all want to believe that there are primordial powers out there and I'm here to tell you that there are. Follow me on a guide to the Wiccan faith and ideals where you'll find out that we believe in tolerance and acceptance above everything else. Let me shake off the mystery and the seriousness that plagues the Wiccan people this day and age. I'm here to give you the straight answers you're looking for.

Thanks again for downloading this book, I hope you enjoy it!

© **Copyright 2015 by Michele Gilbert All rights reserved.**

This document is geared towards providing exact and reliable information in regards to the topic and issue covered. The publication is sold with the idea that the publisher is not required to render accounting, officially permitted, or otherwise, qualified services. If advice is necessary, legal or professional, a practiced individual in the profession should be ordered.

- From a Declaration of Principles which was accepted and approved equally by a Committee of the American Bar Association and a Committee of Publishers and Associations.

In no way is it legal to reproduce, duplicate, or transmit any part of this document in either electronic means or in printed format. Recording of this publication is strictly prohibited and any storage of this document is not allowed unless with written permission from the publisher. All rights reserved.

The information provided herein is stated to be truthful and consistent, in that any liability, in terms of inattention or otherwise, by any usage or abuse of any policies, processes, or directions contained within is the solitary and utter responsibility of the recipient reader. Under no circumstances will any legal responsibility or blame be held against the publisher for any reparation, damages, or monetary loss due to the information herein, either directly or indirectly.

Respective authors own all copyrights not held by the publisher.

The information herein is offered for informational purposes solely, and is universal as so. The presentation of the information is without contract or any type of guarantee assurance.

The trademarks that are used are without any consent, and the publication of the trademark is without permission or backing by the trademark owner. All trademarks and brands within this book are for clarifying purposes only and are the owned by the owners themselves, not affiliated with this document.

What is Wicca?

So you're interested in Wicca, or maybe you've already started your adventure into the big world of one of the oldest religions in the world. It's a noble quest, as is the pursuit of higher knowledge in any religion. For you to continue your journey, or perhaps to start it, you're going to need to begin somewhere and reading is always the best place to start. So here you go.

To be honest, Wicca has, like every religion, evolved over the long years that it has existed. What started as blind paganism and mysticism has adapted and evolved, tearing apart the cruel ambition, dark rituals, and bloody rites that gave it a sense of barbarism. What is left is the enlightened, adapted version of the old ways that have been passed down for ages. Like most religions, there are sects and factions, all of which have ideological differences that distinguish them. But for a brief history on the faith, I will be your esteemed guide through history.

Let's start at the beginning:

In the early twentieth century, the idea of Wicca was first born. Yes, we do trace our roots all the way back to the foundations of religion itself and it is often said that we are one of the oldest faiths because of this. However, to be quite honest, so do most religions. Wicca itself was founded by the meeting of clandestine groups that some call covens. Wait, let me clarify, we call them covens. Our faith existed in silence and in secrecy due to Christian persecution. Originating mostly from European traditions and a resurgence in the mystic arts, it wasn't until the Fifties that we were actually given the name the Craft. This was really the capitalistic boom of our religion, which, from my own personal beliefs, is one of our darker periods. We were much more interested in popularity and attention rather than the pursuit of the Craft.

What you are stepping into now is a much different faith than was previously established in the Sixties and the Seventies after the sensational blossom of our beliefs in the Fifties took root. Today, most Wicca practitioners that you meet are quietly dedicated to the faith and beliefs that they have been taught. Though there are many covens in the world today, meeting and practicing, it is a deeply personalized faith that we follow and it is dedicated to a lot of independent research and development.

Here's what we do not do, or at least to the best of my knowledge. We do not eat babies, we do not worship the devil, and we do not offer human sacrifices. Like I have said before, our faith is extremely popularized by society, no thanks to some of our own members.

Honestly, if you were to meet an average Wiccan on the streets, you probably wouldn't know it. Sure, we draw an element of society, the lost souls, the searching, and the misunderstood. We welcome them and we give them a community, but we're good people and we are not all witches or warlocks.

But, on the other hand, we do practice magic. Yes, I said it. The elephant in the room has been addressed. That's why you're here after all? Isn't that the lure of the Wiccan faith? Magic? The fact that we acknowledge and believe what everyone in their heart secretly knows, that the elements and the forces of the physical and spiritual world are very real and present. Sure, we dabble with primordial forces, but with respect and understanding. No, I cannot turn you into a cat and no I cannot kill you with a spell.

Any true Wicca would rather die than use magic improperly, because there is always a price when it comes to magic.

So, have I piqued your curiosity? Are you interested in knowing more? Then come on in and don't be shy. We'll have a nice little chat and you'll see what it really means to be a Wiccan and I'll tell you about the magic that you know in your heart to be real. I'll give a glimpse at the other side of the world, beyond cell phones and the Internet, where the forests loom and the shadows lurk. There are forces beyond all of us and if you want to know more, I will gladly be your guide.

Concerning Covens:

If you are taking the path that leads you to becoming a Wiccan, you're not like everyone else. You're special, because we do not have Churches, Mosques, or Synagogues on every corner. You will not find temples or university groups, well, you might find a university group or two, but not many. There are a lot of people who like to put on makeup and dress funny and claim to be Wiccans, which makes it hard for newcomers to find a home. If you're serious about becoming a Wiccan or delving into any of the Neopaganism groups, there are many resources.

Thankfully, we've evolved as a people and the Internet has become a wonderful way for us to connect. After all, Wiccans make up less than one percent of the religious community in America, which makes it hard for our brothers and sisters in Nowhere, Nebraska to commune with us. Thanks to the Internet, there's now a way for us to communicate and encourage one another. It's truly a great tool for us to use.

If you're interested in finding a coven near you or a sect that is active in your area, try getting a physical connection before you try the internet, just for the sake of adventure. Find your nearest new age store, every community has one, and speak with someone there. Every new age shop has connections to every aspect of the new age movement which Neopaganism is a huge part of. So if you're interested, go chat before you get online. But if that's not your style and you're still incredibly nervous, then try Witchvox.com. It has a listing for every registered community by state or country. If you don't see your community listed, throw up an ad and see if anyone in your area is interested in meeting and mentoring you.

Now, when it comes to Wiccan groups, there are sects, as I said, like any other religion. You will find that they differ ideologically and that they are influenced by certain members of our founding. It's easy to liken it to popularized Christian sects. John Calvin inspired Calvinism, Martin Luther inspired Lutherans, and John Wesley inspired the Nazarenes. So too do we have our founders and their various sects. Granted, we're not nearly as harsh on the others as Christians are.

Here is a brief list of the common sects you'll find:

Gardnerian:

Founded upon the beliefs of G. Gardner when Wicca popularity was at its height in the Fifties, Gardnerians are by far the most numerous of the Wiccan sects. Established as a matriarchy, Gardnerians are the central figures of the modern Wiccan movement. Most other sects can be seen as off shoots of Gardnerian.

Dianic:

Founded by Margaret Murray in the Twenties, Dianic is a very feminist version of Wicca that is more akin to the Craft. It's very well known that Dianic covens are very political and very active. Some see them as retroactive and misguided; you can be the judge of that.

Alexandrian:

Formed by Alex Sanders at the boom in the Sixties, Sanders started his work in England which spread to the United States. This sect is much more interested in ceremonial magic (or magic, as we refer to it) and is classified as less political or competitive with other religious groups.

Celtic:

Founded on the beliefs of the Druidic and Celtic traditions, the Celtic branch of Wicca, I would say, is the largest growing group. If you have to form up with a Coven, then you're probably going to find that they're more heavily influenced by the Celtic traditions. Many of the members call themselves Druids and are fairly easy to find.

Eclectic:

This is what I would consider myself and this is what I would consider most of the Wiccans that I have come to know. Sure we each have our preferences and our leanings toward a different denomination, but I do not classify myself as neither here nor there. I am a wanderer, picking up what I know from literature and what I learn from others. I would say that the average Wicca would truly consider themselves Eclectic if they do not belong to a true Coven sect.

Locational:

There are several sects that are uniquely adjusted and crafted to the location that they are in. Such as the Strega in Italy, Teutonic in Northern Europe, Pictish in Scotland, or the British Traditionalists in England. These groups are more just locational and focusing on the lore and history of that general region. While beautiful and interesting, they usually just offer unique or different perspectives on all other teachings. They're good to study if you're truly interested in expanding your view of the world.

Now, do not feel like you need to align with any sect. It's not a club mindset. I do not hate Gardnerians or Alexandrians, just like they will not hate me or you. All Wiccans are united through tolerance and a curiosity to discover truth that is relevant to you. You will not find anyone stepping on your beliefs or thinking that you are a fool. We are all about acceptance and understanding.

Tools of the Trade:

If you were to sum up a Catholic Priest's equipment, you'd say a crucifix, holy water, anointing oils, a collar, and maybe a few other things and you'd have yourself a Priest starter kit. Well, if you're looking for that kind of a starter kit for a Wiccan, you're out of luck. There are a few things that every Wiccan will have, but it really depends upon what they're practicing.

Again, there are Wiccans that literally just want a deeper attunement to the world around them and want to read the truths of the earth in nature. They don't practice magic, perform rituals, or do anything like that. There are some that solely practice meditation and crystal work, finding themselves more drawn to Chakra work than anything else. I have a friend that does crystal work and does divination through runes, but considers himself a Wiccan. Again, no magic work. So it really depends upon what you're interested in doing.

But again, there are a few things that we all tend to have and I'll give you a little insight into those.

Talisman:

It's fairly common that every Wiccan or a practitioner in any of the sub-classes of Wicca will have a talisman. Probably the most valued possession that I have is my talisman that I have had for years. My best friend's talisman is his wedding ring and so is his wife's. Mine is an old token of my past that I have carried with me since I was a child. Every day, I have my talisman on me , with me.

A talisman is a sentimental object that has a strong tie or influence from you. It is used to alter negative energy to positive energy, which is vital and imperative for rituals, spells, meditation, and divination. Negative energy is the death of everything that we are trying to do. You'll begin to notice that you're off when you don't have your talisman with you and that will be a very rare day indeed. If you're looking to find your talisman, look at jewelry, which is the most common form a talisman takes. It's easy to wear it or have it with you all the time. Think of what it is that has a mystical tie to you that makes your day just feel off if you don't have it with you.

If you don't have that kind of an object in your life, then you're going to need to find one. They're not necessary, but they're important and we all like to have our own special talisman. I strongly encourage everyone to have a talisman. It's pretty much the key to any form of divination work or cleansing your aura.

Candles:

If there's another item that I'd say you'd see any one practicing magic would have, it's got to be candles. Every spell calls for candles, especially different or unique candles that are specific to any form of the spell that you're casting. Colors are of great significance when it comes to a spell. For example, using red candles instead of white candles will produce a different outcome to the spell that you're trying to cast and may even cause your spell to fail. Again, like I said, you're going to find candles with pretty much every spell that's brought along.

Crystals:

It's pretty fundamental to understand how meditation and auras work when trying to cast a spell. For those unacquainted with crystals and the power that they have, there are countless books that you can find to teach you on the subject. A real quick overview is that crystals are primordial energy from the earth and have different effects upon our energy and aura. Crystals can greatly enhance your natural gifts and augment that which you're trying to accomplish. Whether you're using your crystals for meditation and communing purposes or for runes, crystals are fairly common with anyone who is practicing the magic arts of Wicca.

Salt:

There are so many spells that call for salts that it's dizzying. I think that I use more salt than I use candles. Salt is a great material for rituals as well and you'll find different kinds of salts out there. Again, while many spells require various exotic and domestic ingredients, you'll go through a lot of salt. It's just a common ingredient. Of course, it's hard to find black salt just anywhere. You'll find yourself frequenting new age shops quite often once you begin your journey down the Wiccan path.

Those four items are pretty much what I use most and what I would suggest a beginning Wiccan to invest in. Of course, you're going to need to research the crystals and do some experiments with them. Any spell is going to call for more ingredients than just salt and candles, and you're going to have to buy a lot more. Most items that you need are going to be readily available at new age shops and if they don't have it, most have venders that will get you what you need. Again, these are just four basic items. If you're looking to start right now without spending any money, consider meditating and finding your totem. It's going to prove to be important to you later on.

A note on Athames and chalices. There are a lot of Wiccans that are very hard core, very deep in the covens, and very bent on rituals. They perform many rituals on the Sabbats and they have a lot of elixirs that they craft for those rituals. Unless you're really bent on getting into a coven and really developing yourself in the coven, athames are pretty pointless. I'd also suggest letting your coven bestow an athame upon you.

Also, a lot of people inform me that a pentacle is very necessary to perform a ritual. I'd say yes, if you also have a time machine and go back to the seventies and the eighties. Maybe it's just a location thing for me, but I don't know a lot of people that actually own a pentacle anymore. I have many friends who have a pentacle tattoo, but that's about it. Wait and see if you're really going to utilize it if you're practices before you buy one. I know that back in the day they were pretty big, mostly because they were a propaganda piece.

Rites, Rituals, Spells, and Practices:

Now, what exactly do we do? Well, that's a complex question. That's like asking a Muslim what it is they do or a Buddhist what they do? It's a complex metaphysical study and community fellowship that brings us together in the pursuit of the greater purposes and meanings in life. Of course, there is a lot more mysticism surrounding our beliefs, but I wouldn't say that it's any different than any other church or faith. We congregate and we have our traditions that we pass down from elders to the newer members. All Wiccans are about belonging, acceptance, and the pursuit of knowledge. We all hunger for that which we seek and that is to understand the Universe or the God and Goddess. It all depends upon what you feel called to pursue.

I'm sorry it's not all orgies and goat bleedings.

Actually, no I'm not. At least the bleeding part.

For those of you looking for the crazy sex stuff, I won't tease you anymore or drag you on. Yes, there is a sexual practice known as the Great Rite which is a symbolic rite that is performed to signify the unity of the God and the Goddess. Have I known covens to basically turn this into an orgy for religious purposes? Yes. Have I known covens that do not? Yes. Mostly the Great Rite is performed with established couples and no one is ever forced to have sex and there is nothing close to rape involved. So we can settle that nagging question for some of you once and for all. It is basically turning your intimate, sexual experience into a religious rite for deeper understanding. That's all. Nothing weird or creepy, I assure you.

We do party a lot and there's some significant ceremony and traditions behind them, but mostly they're great community times and events. It's known as the Wheel of the Year. We divide the year up into Sabbats, or what some might call holidays, I guess. That's probably the best way to explain it to you. These Sabbats are different with each coven and there's significance to each of them, depending upon what you worship and seek to understand. Overall, I usually attend as many Sabbats as I can, just to show my support. It's a good way to show unity with our brothers and sisters. See if you have a local gathering for one and show up. You'll have a good time and you're going to be welcomed for sure.

Now, for spells and rituals, I'm going to tell you that there is a very nit-picky difference that many Wiccans will rip my head off for trivializing, but basically, they're the same thing. I'm going to tell you that if you came up to me asking me to perform a banishment spell and another person came up asking me to perform a banishment ritual, I would be performing the same thing. Sure, there are traditional differences, but I know what you want and I'm going to do what you ask. Ask the wrong Wiccan and they'll give you a lecture for hours about the subtle nuances and differences between the two. Lucky for you, I am not one of them.

I suppose I should also mention chants for our Celtic brothers and sisters out there performing the Druidic arts. The Druids are famous for their chants. When the Romans occupied Celtic territory, the Druids would slip out of the forests at night and perform chants upon their forts and outposts. Very spooky stuff, but these days, Druids are a lot more peaceful and in tune with nature. Again, I'm going to maybe get in trouble for this, but I consider Chants the Celtic way of saying spell. Send all complaints and diatribes to my agent.

The last kind of specific rituals or spells that I would like to address are charms. Charms are blessed objects that are designed for a purpose in mind. Such as a wealth charm, a beauty charm, a success charm, or any other kind of charm that might be used to augment the wearer. If you're a bloodthirsty capitalist, this might be the route for you. People will pay top dollar for a charm that doesn't look ridiculous. Of course, it's also a trade rampant with charlatans, so good luck.

Now, before we get into the types of spells and some simple spells, we need to have a chat. You are not Harry Potter and you are not Gandalf. You cannot become Voldemort and you cannot abuse primordial powers for your own will without a cost. Understand me that there are very powerful people set to oversee that you do not get away with anything violent, cruel, or excessively selfish. Mostly magic itself will not let you get away with it. There is a price and a cost for everything that you do and it is monstrous. Sure, a lightning bolt might not kill you, but I've known people to suddenly have a very unfortunate audit for performing improper magic. I've known people to lose their jobs suddenly because they're performing foul magic.

So I will answer that question too. Yes, there is dark magic out there. It is a thing and there are those that practice it. But they are weak people who are consumed with troubles and stupidity. You do not want to be one of them, because all good magic is so much better. Love, wealth, success, courage, protection, and beauty are all on our side, so join us and don't waste your time looking up curses and vexes. It's a waste of your time. Trust in the Universe and it will be your bastion of vengeance.

Now, where were we?

Types of Spells:

Again, yes, I'm sorry to interrupt your pursuit of the magic arts, but I feel you need to be warned. There are lots of spells out there and there is a lot of literature for you to read. You're going to find that there are so many books out there that it might get troublesome for you to find truth in any of this. I'm telling you now to contact anyone in person that might help you on your journey. They will help you discern the difference between Barnes & Noble charlatans and the true sources of wisdom. Again, if you try a spell and you find that it doesn't work, don't blame Wicca, blame the spell. Keep searching and keep uncovering the truth. You will find the spell that works.

If you show up to a new age shop, you're going to find a lot of different types of magic that you could possibly perform. There is not a universal magic that everyone taps into. It all depends upon something different. Druidic Chants are not the same as Hoodoo and you should know that up front. Don't be trying to do everything at once. Again, this is most successful when you consult someone who is practicing to guide you through all of this.

Now, it's time for the basic overall view of different kinds of magic's.

Astral Projection

In the ancient days, Astral Projection was often confused with channeling and it's often considered a deeper form of meditation or meditational magic. There's a difference, and I'll get to that later. Astral Projection is having an out of body experience with a purpose. You are searching for something, sending your spirit through the spirit world or physical world to hunt for something. Lots of spells invoke astral projection and it is super terrifying to experience at first. It is a strange magic that is often confusing. The spirit world often takes on the views we inflict upon it. So often it is hard to know if you are really seeing the physical world or if you're travelling the spirit world and shaping it as you go. I know a woman who offers her services as a guide for those first trying Astral Projection for the first time. I would consider finding a guide to help you in your initial journeys.

Banishing Spells:

Banishment is a very powerful spell that is often taught to those looking to learn magic for the first time. Banishing can be used for many purposes, but a lot of the time, it's used to redress wrongs in the physical world. Banishment can remove negative energies, dark spiritual presences, and hurts that have lingered and festered for years. Most banishing's that I've attended have been used on properties that have just been purchased. Not as glamorous as you'd like to imagine, but it's always useful.

Beauty Spells:

Who doesn't want to look beautiful? Believe it or not, but vanity and beauty are some of the oldest spells that we have. Don't get this mistaken for love spells. If you're looking to have someone fall in love with you, you want a love spell, not a beauty spell. A beauty spell is means you're looking for influence over people in a positive manner. People are more inclined to listen to someone with a beautiful appearance than someone normal or unattractive.

Blessings:

This is what you're going to find most often in any Wiccan circle, because in the end, we are all about helping people. We can find you blessings for everything. Blessings are simple spells that are often very easy to practice and master because any magic that is mean to bless someone is always easier to invoke than other magic's. Blessings are wonderful, sweet spells that you give to people freely without anything in return.

Charms:

Charms are a combination of different kinds of spells that are focused on talismans or objects that can be given, or more likely sold, to a person. There are a lot of Wiccans that practice magic just for the sake of charms. Whether they give these charms freely or with a cost, that's on them. There are charms for pretty much everything. From courage to luck to love; you'll find a charm for whatever problem you have and hopefully it works. I think that charm magic is one of the most powerful magic's you can partake in because you're not keeping the magic to yourself. It's a selfless magic, unless you're making money off it, of course.

Cleansings:

These are often confused with banishment spells and I suppose I understand the similarity. But they are different. Cleansings are scrubbing an area clean where banishment usually involves chasing something out or keeping something away. Cleansings are getting away that residual presence, even if it's faint. Again, I've seen this mostly used with material possessions and property.

Divination:

Honestly, I think this is the most common form of magic that is practiced in daily life of most Wiccans, especially those really into crystal work. Divination is considered a ritual and is used to discern the future or meaning of things through the use of signs and symbols. Most commonly, you're going to see this with runes and I practice it quite often. Divination is just a glimpse into what the future has in store without spoiling the form and shape of things to come. We just know the intention of the Universe's path.

Dream Rituals:

Even as I write this, I'm hesitant to include it on this list, because I'm not certain that I believe that Dream work is actually magic. I feel that it's a deeper form of meditation. Lucid dreaming is a very real thing that is being studied by psychologists and I'm not convinced that it's magic, nor did I ever really think that it was magic. But, there are many who do, so I won't exclude it. Mostly, it's exploring the dream world with full consciousness to discern truths about yourself and the world. It's powerful and it's very interesting to experience.

Exorcism Rituals:

Though we do not have the same beliefs as the Christian duality in the spirit world, we do acknowledge that there are very real and powerful forces at work in the world and we look to keep those spirits from harming people. For that, we have exorcism rituals that help remove dark spirits from people that have been sent either through poor choices, dark magic, or just random happenstance. I have never seen an exorcism ritual, nor have I ever found a point where it was needed. Though, I have heard stories and I have heard tales of its use.

Fertility Rituals:

This is a common ritual, which honestly, I've found to be a reason for people looking to conceive just to have a blessing when they have sex. It's a traditional ritual that's used to bless the conception of a child. It's nothing sinister or overly provocative. It's just a means to bless a couple trying to have a child and to encourage them to conceive. There are fertility charms that are often given to those trying to start a family.

Goddess Rituals:

Consider the Great Rite that I told you about earlier to be lumped into this category because it's done for the benefit and the acknowledgement of the God and the Goddess. You're rarely see men performing rituals or spells in the name of the God, but you'll see it quite often with Dianic covens to perform rituals in the name of the Goddess. Remember that most covens are matriarchal and women have a very strong leadership presence. You'll see people performing a ritual every now and again in honor of the Goddess, which is very interesting.

Healing Spells:

I've got to say that this ranks up there with the top five kinds of spells that I perform and I see performed most often. You see people practicing healing magic all the time and it's the most common magic that you'll find being worked among the public. These spells are extremely self-explanatory and that's that they are used to help people heal physically or spiritually. They're often considered blessings and rightly so. Learn healing spells as often as you can. You'll be using them in abundance.

Invocation Rituals:

This is another ritual that I haven't seen too often, maybe it's a location thing, but here in the northwest, I don't see a lot of invocations other than to the Goddess. Invocation is often used to call spirits or beings to your presence in order to learn for them or to benefit from their presence. A lot of superstitious people will tell you that it's dangerous to perform invocation rituals due to trickster spirits looking to confuse your or lead you astray. Again, I don't know enough people that invoke to get a serious answer on this.

Job Spells:

Ah, yes, the spells requested by the desperate and the lazy. I do not count job spells as anything other than lies. I'm going to catch a lot of flak for this, but it's fodder for the weak minded. If you come to me for a spell to ensure that you get the job you're going to interview for, just nail the interview. If you're in a contest with others, I'll give you a luck charm or spell, but I think job spells are a bunch of lies, but a lot of people believe in them, so they make the list.

Love Spells, Charms, and Rituals:

Now, next to beauty, love has to be the most commonly invoked magic of all time. People are always to trying to get the cutting edge in the hand of the one that they love. I think that love spells are very powerful and should not be used flippantly and I make sure that the person I'm casting it on behalf of us very committed to the idea of taking care of the one they love before its cast. Messing with the hearts of people is not to be taken lightly and make sure you're ready for the consequences of casting this spell, performing this ritual, or utilizing this charm. The Universe will certainly answer unkindly if you screw it up.

Prosperity Spells:

I don't know if I truly trust in prosperity spells because I don't know an honest Wiccan who would ever use magic for such a selfish purpose as to obtain prosperity through physical wealth. The spells do exist, but I will never perform one because I do not belief utilizing magic to such selfish reasons

Protection Spells:

Here we go again with the top five most common spells performed. Protection spells are often used on, well, pretty much everything. No matter what you have value of, there is a spell that will keep it safe from harm. Often, protection spells are paired with other spells that are used to cleanse or banish negative energy before protection is applied. I've performed quite a few protection spells than any other spell.

Psychic Rituals:

I don't have a lot of experience in the psychic arts, mostly because I don't think I'm very sensitive to this type of magic or power. But, there are a lot of people that perform rituals to help boost their psychic power before meditation sessions.

Sabbat Rituals:

Consider these more like ceremonies than actual spells, but they do have power and are often invocation spells, but they merit their own category, because they're used specifically during Sabbats. They're never used outside of ceremonies and are truly unique.

<u>Truth Spells:</u>

You'll find truth spells are fairly common too, but I don't think I've ever found a reason to use one. I know that some Wiccans use them to get the truth from a spouse or partner that they're certain is keeping something form them. Be careful what you wish for, that's all I have to say.

I know that it's not in alphabetical order, but I'm putting it last because I know a lot of people who don't consider it an actual magic, but rather an act of communing, but I think that it merits mentioning so I'm giving it a special place here at the end.

Earth Magic is the most selfless form of magic that I know, because it isn't applicable to people, other than a symptom of the magic's effects. Earth Magic is often used to beseech the Goddess to help heal the earth and to understand what is happening with the earth. Constantly many Wiccans are caught up in the environment, feeling the magic that flows freely, letting it speak to them and fill them as they are present in nature. It's powerful and it's becoming more and more popular among Wiccans.

That's the Show Folks:

So that's what there is to the basic truths of Wicca and a classification of the spells that I've learned about, heard about, or seen used in my travels. I also hope that I gave you an understanding of what it means to be a Wiccan and cleared up some of the mysticism that has plagued our faith for centuries. We are a people of tolerance and acceptance and we are not about persecution or cursing others on our own behalf.

If you've read this book and you think that it's nothing but a bunch of hocus pocus and hog wash, then that's your opinion and I respect it and understand why you might think that. Remember that once I was not a Wiccan either and no one is born with the beliefs they come to hold true. Perhaps one day you'll understand differently. I do ask that you don't persecute or insult those of us who do practice in your area. We're not going to curse your home and family and we're not going to burn your church or temple down. We're just good people looking out for the betterment of humanity, just like you are.

If you've read this book and you think that you might be interested in more, great! We're out there and we're definitely willing to talk with you and explain more to you. Read more books, there are plenty of them out there for you and you'll be able to grow more and more on your own if you're too scared to come find us. But I hope you do. Go to your nearest new age shop and start talking. They're all extremely friendly and more than willing to chat with you. Maybe one day we'll meet and we'll have a great time together.

But no matter what you believe, may the Goddess bless you in all your ways.

Conclusion

Before you go, I'd like to say thank you for purchasing my book.

I know you could have picked so many other books to read on Wicca. But you took a chance on me.

So A Big thanks for downloading this book and reading it all the way to completion.

Now I would like to ask a *small* favor.

Could you please take a minute or two to leave a review for this book on Amazon?

Click here

The feedback will help me continue to publish more kindle books that will help people to get better results in their lives.

And if you found it helpful in anyway then please let me know :-)

Preview of My New Book

Talk to the Hand

I don't know about you, but when I watch shows like *Lie to Me* or *Sherlock*, so often, I really, really wish that I could be that good. Heck, after I watched *The Mentalist* for the first time, I was studying everyone. I stared at footprints trying to see if I could tell whether the person walking was right handed or left handed. Not only is this super impractical for me as an actual skill, but it's super addicting. The thing is, it's all about studying people and watching them, but there's a science to it. I may not be out there catching criminals red handed for having a nervous tell, but it has helped me read situations and understand things that I previously missed.

So sure, you might not catch your arch-nemesis, but you might be able to understand things a little better with a little study of body language. And that's why I'm here. Body language is not just for detectives out there looking to catch murderers and thieves. Body language is the key to understanding the unspoken words that our body is communicating so heavily without our knowledge. Not only will this help you understand and relate to people better, but it'll make it so that you are aware of your own presence to others.

Nonverbal communication makes up the majority of our communication and most of us are clueless to the actual comprehension and understanding of it. That means that those who do not invest time in learning what to say in our nonverbal appearance are missing so much. But the truth is, we don't miss all of it. We have come to silently absorb and understand nonverbal communication, regardless of whether we know it or not. It's the art of learning to understand something we already know and to heighten our understanding and acceptance of what's being communicated to us. It's tricky, I know, but it's not impossible to understand.

What I'm going to tell you in this book is going to make sense to you and a lot of it is going to feel familiar, like you already knew that. Well, the reason for that is that you you've been picking up these silent transmissions for years, you just haven't acknowledged them or put a name to some of the habits you've already taught yourself.

So stick around and start to see if you can't agree or relate to some of the information you're going to receive. But more importantly, I want to address your homework before we start getting into the gritty, deep stuff. For instance, I want you to start watching people around you.

Observation is the birth of understanding and without a true sense of observance or a keen eye for noticing the little things, you're not going to pick up on some of these traits. When someone is talking to you, you're going to need to start watching them. Notice how they're standing, note the posture, have you looked at their eyes, what about the overall harmony of their face, and what are they doing with their hands? All of these things need to be running through your mind to really catch what is being conveyed to you. But not just watching their body, note the tones they're using, and the words that they're selecting. These are all going to tell you what sort of body language comes with certain attitudes and emotions. It all ties together and it is all relevant when it comes to understanding body language. So start opening your eyes and let's have a look at what they're trying to say to you.

Are you ready?

Weapons of Mass Induction

Though Sherlock Holmes often touts his use of deductive reasoning, it is actually the opposite that we're going to focus on with you, because right now, you're a student. For those of you that do not know, inductive reasoning starts with observations that slowly build a pattern that you will then form into a hypothesis until it is proven right or wrong. If you're right, then you have a theory.

For example, Kayla touches her hair a lot when she talks to Hot Mike, but not when she's talking to anyone else. So, every time I see Kayla talking to Hot Mike and she's touching her hair, that might be a cue that she likes Hot Mike. So, until I'm proven wrong, I'm certain that I have a theory that when a woman likes a man, she'll touch her hair unconsciously.

Viola, you have just jumped from observation to theory until proven wrong. Of course, when you're Sherlock Holmes level, you'll be using the art of deductive reasoning which starts at a theory and then tested with a hypothesis and observations until you have a conclusion. I think it's time for another example to prove this one to you.

Click Here To Read The Rest of

Body Language 101

What A Person's Body Language Is Really Telling You... And How You Can Use It To Your Advantage

P.S. You'll find many more books like this and others under my name Michele Gilbert.

Don't miss them... here is a short list.

Wicca: The Ultimate Beginners Guide For Witches and Warlocks: Learn Wicca Magic

The Introvert's Advantage: The Introverts Guide To Succeeding In An Extrovert World

Stop Playing Mind Games: How To Free Yourself Of Controlling And Manipulating Relationships

Instant Charisma: A Quick And Easy Guide To Talk, Impress, And Make Anyone Like You

Chakras: Understanding The 7 Main Chakras For Beginners: The Ultimate Guide To Chakra Mindfulness, Balance and Healing

Practicing Mindfulness: Living in the moment through Meditation: Everyday Habits and Rituals to help you achieve inner peace

Adrenal Fatigue: What Is Adrenal Fatigue Syndrome And How To Reset Your Diet And Your Life

Sleep Tight: Overcome Insomnia and Sleep Disorders for a better more restful sleep!

Stop Back Pain Now!: Back Pain Remedies and Treatments so you can live a pain free life!

The Arthritis Pain Cure: How to find Arthritis Pain Relief and live a happy pain free life!

The Headache Pain Cure: How to find Headache Pain Relief and live a happy Pain Free Life!

Stop Panic Attacks and Anxiety Disorders without Drugs Now!: Overcome Panic, Stress and Anxiety and live a happy pain free life!

The Breakup Recovery Guide: Advice for Surviving Heartbreak, Letting Go and Thriving in an exciting new life!

The Friendship Guide to Finding Friends Forever: How to Find, Make and Keep Quality Friendships After your Breakup

How To Stop Being Jealous And Insecure: Overcome Insecurity And Relationship Jealousy

Psychic Development: Your Guide To Unlocking Your Psychic Abilities

The Mind Of A Sociopath: Your Guide to Understanding The Anti-Social Personality Disorder of Sociopaths

About Michele Gilbert

Michele Gilbert was born and raised in Brooklyn, New York. Drawn to literature and writing at a young age, she enrolled at Brooklyn College and majored in English. After graduation Michele did not begin writing immediately, instead she embarked on a career in the finance industry and spent the next thirty years on Wall Street.

Serendipity struck when she least expected it. After ending a long-term relationship, Michele found herself lost and unsure what the future held. She began to read books on grief and loss, looking for answers. Those led her to delve deeper into the Law of Attraction and its power. What resulted was remarkable. Not only had she begun to heal, she had also rekindled her former love of writing and discovered her life's purpose.

The years have taken her through many twists and turns, but she learned valuable lessons along the way. Today she publishes books-mostly self-help and metaphysical in nature-and feels compelled to share her knowledge with those facing similar experiences. Her greatest hope is to inspire others and show them ways to overcome adversity and gracefully accept life's inevitable low points.

Going forward, she plans to incorporate more teachings of self-help, finance and meditation. Regular meditation is very beneficial to her progress as she forges a new life. Morning rituals and positive incantations are other practices Michele embraces; they are very restorative in daily life.

As an avid hiker, Michele and fellow club members often hike the picturesque Jersey Pine Barrens. She is a history buff, voracious reader, baseball fanatic and a foodie. She also proudly supports Trout Unlimited-a national non-profit organization dedicated to conserving, protecting and restoring North America's Coldwater fisheries and their watersheds.

Michele currently resides forty minutes from Atlantic City and the Jersey Shore. She makes her home with a Blue Russian rescue cat named Jersey, though she isn't exactly sure who rescued who.

Michele really enjoys publishing books that can make a difference in people's lives. If you have any suggestions or would like to have a specific topic covered in a future book, please send an email to michelegilbertbooks@gmail.com and we will get back to you.

Thanks for reading!

www.ingramcontent.com/pod-product-compliance
Lightning Source LLC
Chambersburg PA
CBHW050926290526
45792CB00002B/899